T0008813

FOOTBALL'S GREATEST

MYTHS AND LEGENDS

by Elliott Smith

CAPSTONE PRESS
a capstone imprint

Published by Capstone Press, an imprint of Capstone
1710 Roe Crest Drive, North Mankato, Minnesota 56003
capstonepub.com

SPORTS ILLUSTRATED KIDS is a trademark of ABG-SI LLC. Used with permission.

Library of Congress Cataloging-in-Publication Data
Names: Smith, Elliott, 1976– author.
Title: Football's greatest myths and legends / by Elliott Smith.
Description: North Mankato, Minnesota : Capstone Press, [2023] | Series: Sports illustrated
  kids: sports greatest myths and legends | Includes bibliographical references and index. |
  Audience: Ages 9-11 | Audience: Grades 4-6
Summary: "Why is Green Bay, Wisconsin, nicknamed "Titletown?" Does "icing" the kicker of
  an opposing team actually work? Do sewer systems in some cities really get flooded
  during halftime on Super Bowl Sunday? Dig in to get the real stories behind these and
  other great football myths and legends!"-- Provided by publisher.
Identifiers: LCCN 2022025127 (print) | LCCN 2022025128 (ebook) | ISBN 9781669003571
  (hardcover) | ISBN 9781669040293 (paperback) | ISBN 9781669003533 (pdf) | ISBN
  9781669003557 (kindle edition)
Subjects: LCSH: Football—Miscellanea—Juvenile literature. | Football—History—Juvenile
  literature. | Legends—Juvenile literature.
Classification: LCC GV950.7 .S588 2023 (print) | LCC GV950.7 (ebook) | DDC 796.330973—
  dc23/eng/20220502
LC record available at https://lccn.loc.gov/2022025127
LC ebook record available at https://lccn.loc.gov/2022025128

Editorial Credits
Aaron Sautter, editor; Bobbie Nuytten, designer; Donna Metcalf, media researcher;
Whitney Schaefer, production specialist

Image Credits
Associated Press: Chris Park/Invision for EA Sports, 7, Tony Tomsic, cover right; Getty
Images: Cliff Welch, 19, Dustin Bradford, 11, James Flores, 27, Jamie Squire, 9, Michael
Longo/Icon Sportswire, 10, Mike Ehrmann, 15, Nate Fine/NFL, 23, Norm Hall, 13, Philip
Pacheco, 21, Sports Studio Photos, 4; Shutterstock: Grigvovan, 22; Sports Illustrated:
Damian Strohmeyer, 17, 24, 26, Erick W. Rasco, 25, 8, John Iacono, 28, Robert Beck, cover
left, Simon Bruty, 29

All internet sites appearing in back matter were available and accurate when this book was
sent to press.

Table of Contents

Words in **bold** are in the glossary.

What's in a name?

Football is a great game. Millions of fans love the sport. It began in 1869. Many football **myths** have grown over the years.

One legend is about the ball itself. It's often called a pigskin. But footballs were never made from pig skin.

Footballs were once made from pig **bladders**. The bladders were stuffed with straw. Then they were covered in leather. Today, the inner balls are made from rubber.

Let's dig into some other big football myths.

Video Game Jinx

Madden NFL video games are very popular. People love them! Being on the game's cover is a big honor for National Football League (NFL) players. But some people think it's a **curse**. They think the players always get hurt or have bad seasons.

Former running back Barry Sanders was on the cover of *Madden NFL 25*.

Some Madden cover players have been hurt in the past. But many have done well. Patrick Mahomes was on *Madden NFL 20*. He won the Super Bowl that season! Tom Brady was on *Madden NFL 22*. He threw a career-high 5,316 yards that year.

Ice, Ice Baby

Kickers are important players in close games. Just one **field goal** can give a team a win. But some coaches like to take last-second **timeouts**. This is called "icing" the kicker. They hope to make the kicker nervous so he might miss.

Some fans think icing the kicker is a myth. But the **stats** show it's not. Without a timeout, kickers hit 81 percent of their kicks. But it's different with a timeout. Then just 68 percent of kicks succeed.

FACT

Alabama coach Paul "Bear" Bryant truly earned his nickname. He wrestled a bear when he was 13 years old!

Vikings kicker Greg Joseph (#1) misses a game-winning kick against the Arizona Cardinals.

The 6th-Round GOAT

Some fans think Tom Brady is the G.O.A.T. That means the Greatest of All Time. Many people think Brady had to be a top pick in the 2000 NFL **Draft**. But that's wrong. He wasn't chosen until number 199.

15

In college, Brady played quarterback for the University of Michigan. He started his last two years. Brady thought he was ready for the pros. But NFL scouts weren't so sure.

FACT

Tom Brady has won seven Super Bowls. That's more than any player in history!

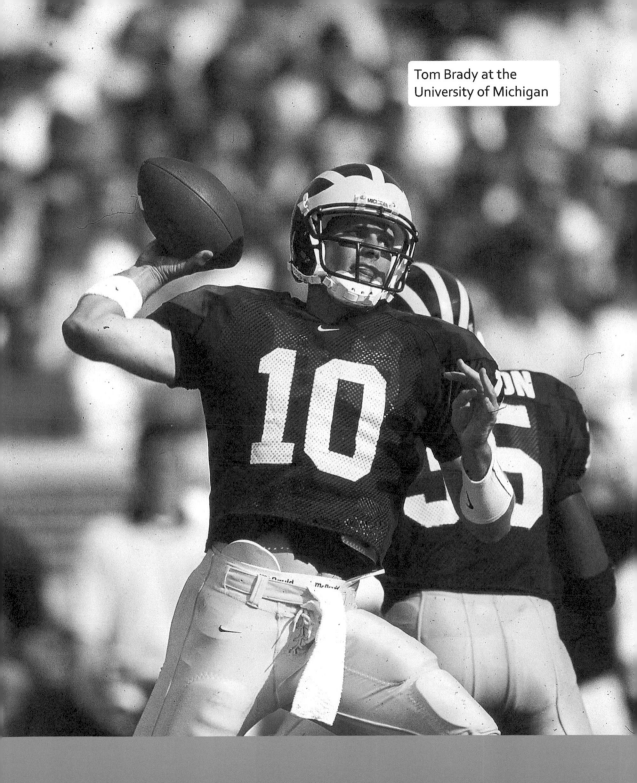

Tom Brady at the University of Michigan

In the draft, six quarterbacks were picked before Brady. Only two started more than three games. Meanwhile, Brady has been to 10 Super Bowls.

Super Bowl Flush?

Fans love to watch the Super Bowl. Many throw big parties. During halftime, many fans run to use the bathroom. Do all those flushing toilets cause big problems?

Some say that city **sewers** can't handle the extra water. But this isn't true. People do use more water during halftime. But there's no proof the extra flushing floods the sewers.

FACT

World War II led to a lack of football players. In 1943, the Pittsburgh Steelers and Philadelphia Eagles combined teams. They played that season as the Steagles.

The Real Champs

The Pittsburgh Steelers have six Super Bowl wins. So do the New England Patriots. They're tied for the most Super Bowl **titles**.

But the NFL began in 1920. The Super Bowl didn't start until 1967. There were 46 years of champs before then. Do any teams have more than six titles?

One team sits at the top of the list. The Green Bay Packers are the all-time champs. They have 13 total NFL titles. This includes four Super Bowl wins. That's how Green Bay earned the nickname of "Titletown."

FACT

Quarterback Bart Starr (#15) led the Packers to win Super Bowl I and II.

Two teams follow the Packers. The Chicago Bears have nine NFL titles. Only one win came in a Super Bowl. The New York Giants own eight titles. Four of them were Super Bowl wins.

The Bears beat the Patriots in Super Bowl XX.

The New York Giants defeated the Patriots in Super Bowl XLVI.

FACT

The Cleveland Browns have four NFL titles. So do the Detroit Lions. But neither team has ever played in a Super Bowl.

Glossary

bladder (BLAD-uhr)—a sac inside the body that holds urine

curse (KURS)—a spell or charm that supposedly causes harm or misfortune to happen to someone

draft (DRAFT)—an event in which college athletes are picked to join a pro sports team

field goal (FEELD GOHL)—a play in which the ball is kicked through the goalposts for three points

myth (MITH)—a false idea that many people believe

sewer (SOO-ur)—a system of underground drains and pipes used to carry wastewater away from homes and buildings

stats (STATS)—short for statistics; numbers, such as wins and losses, that represent the performance of a player or team

timeout (TYME-out)—a brief pause or break in a game

title (TYE-tuhl)—an award given to the champion of a sport

Read More

Berglund, Bruce. *Football GOATs: The Greatest Athletes of All Time*. North Mankato, MN: Capstone Press, 2022.

Lowe, Alexander. *G.O.A.T. Football Running Backs*. Mankato, MN: Lerner Publications, 2023.

Pryor, Shawn. *Football's Sickest Sacks!* North Mankato, MN: Capstone Press, 2021.

Internet Sites

NFL Play 60
gonoodle.com/tags/ZwmZ5Y/nfl-play-60

Pro Football Hall of Fame
profootballhof.com/

Sports Illustrated Kids: Football
sikids.com/football

Super Bowl History
history.com/topics/sports/super-bowl-history

Index

About the Author

Elliott Smith is a former sports reporter who covered athletes in all sports from high school to the pros. He is one of the authors of the Natural Thrills series about extreme outdoor sports. In his spare time, he likes playing sports with his two children, going to the movies, and adding to his collection of Pittsburgh Steelers memorabilia.